Beggar in the Everglades

poems by

Diana Woodcock

Finishing Line Press
Georgetown, Kentucky

Beggar in the Everglades

ACKNOWLEDGMENTS

I am grateful to the editors of the following journals, in which some of these poems first appeared, at
times in slightly different versions.

Carpe Articulum Literary Review: "Elegy for Guy Bradley."
Connotation Press: An Online Artifact: "Everglades History Lesson One;" "Grassy River;" and
    "Pa-hay-okee."
Copperfield Review: "Returning."
Crab Orchard Review: "In the Company of Alligators."
ECOTHEE: Ecological Theology and Environmental Ethics: "Beggar in the Everglades," "Kin to All of
    Nature," "Pa-hay-okee," and "Tattered Battlefield, National Treasure."
Flyway: A Literary Review: "Beggar in the Everglades."
Hobble Creek Review: "Murder in the Everglades;" "Off-Season in Paradise."
ISLE: Interdisciplinary Studies in Literature and Environment, forthcoming: "Pa-hay-okee," and
    "Celestial Cathedral."
Jellyfish Whispers: "Edge of a Sawgrass Prairie."
National Park Service, Through Your Eyes (website): "In the Company of Alligators," Beggar in the
    Everglades," and "Everglades: Day One."
Poised in Flight Anthology, Kind of a Hurricane Press,: "Together We Watch."
Portland Review: "Everglades: Day One."
Quiddity: "Existence is Light."
Saw Palm: Florida Literature and Art (Places to Stand feature): "First Sunset, "Anhinga Trail,"
    "Mahogany Hammock," "Shark Valley," and "Shark Valley, Near Noon."
Southern Women's Review: "If You Doubt" (print, on-line at www.SouthernWomensReview.com).
Spillway: "Kin to All of Nature."
Wild Things, Outrider Press: "Love at First Sighting."

"In the Company of Alligators," Beggar in the Everglades," and "Everglades: Day One" were chosen by
the National Park Service for inclusion in its Through Your Eyes web multi-media exhibitions (2013).
These three poems also were featured in the AIRIE Collection exhibit, December 1-31, 2011 in the
Ernest F. Coe Visitor Center Gallery, Everglades National Park and at the O'Miami Poetry Festival in
April 2011. "Grassy River" received an Honorable Mention in the 2009 Ortonville CreekFest Poetry
Contest. "Last Breath" won 3rd place in the 2009 Poetry Competition sponsored by the Roanoke
Valley Branch of the National League of American Pen Women.

Editor: Christen Kincaid
Cover Art: Paula Baxter
Author Photo: Miles Lowry

Printed in the USA on acid-free paper.
Order online: www.finishinglinepress.com
                also available on amazon.com

Author inquiries and mail orders:
Finishing Line Press
P. O. Box 1626
Georgetown, Kentucky 40324
U. S. A.

Table of Contents

Love at First Sighting...1

Everglades, Day One...2

In the Company of Alligators....................................4

Beggar in the Everglades 6

Existence is Light...8

Elegy for Guy Bradley..10

Grassy River...12

Off-Season in Paradise...14

Envious...16

Celestial Cathedral...18

Returning...19

American Alligator..21

Everglades' Keystone Species 22

If You Doubt..24

Mercury..26

Edge of a Sawgrass Prairie.....................................27

Everglades History Lesson One.............................29

Kin to All of Nature..31

Pa-hay-okee 33

Tattered Battlefield, National Treasure.................35

Together We Watch...37

Murder in the Everglade 38

Shark Valley..39

Shark Valley, Near Noon...41

First Sunset, Anhinga Trail 43

Facing Aridity...45

*for all the endangered ones
whose home is the River of Grass*

LOVE AT FIRST SIGHTING

Love at first sight,
or sighting to be precise.
Infused with desire to enter

into each life—be accepted
by crocodile, spider lily,
sphinx moth in mangrove swamp,

alligator under its pond
apple tree in Taylor Slough.
Everywhere water flowing

imperceptibly toward sea.
Even sawgrass captivating me,
though I kept my distance.

From the first encounter,
no resistance—only a vague
sense of remembrance,

as if I'd known it all my life.
Royal palms like cathedral spires
marking this haven of heaven.

EVERGLADES: DAY ONE

Here for just one month, I'll say it
at the outset: I won't go
until I see the snakes King and Indigo.
Although ultimate goal's not merely
to see but become one with it—
spend my days just being in its midst—
this the gist of it:

lazing away a part of each day dozing
under pond apple trees with alligator,
pig frogs chanting their lullabies nearby;
drifting with Florida gar, unconcerned
with going far; staying alert, finding a way
to interpret sloughs and solution holes—
engage with quiet surfaces, June's subtleties;
creeping as graciously as the grassy river
flowing south, marveling at what
each component's all about.

No doubt hope's voice rings louder here
than that of despair's. I hear it everywhere:
sense of wonder reawakened, sense of awe
as eyes have taken in vast expanses of saw-
grass. Listening with ears and heart, hearing
Earth whispering and gesturing—wind swaying
blade-sharp sedges—then speaking loudly,
clearly in roars of male alligators, snorts
of pig frogs, harsh calls of marsh birds.

I have come, as Job suggested,* asking
panther, anhinga, gar fish, alligator to teach me.
Loosening my hair as Li Po instructed, I linger
where water flows imperceptibly to sea
though we cut it with swords. ** I wake and sleep
in its arms, stand quiet as a stalking bittern
blending into the wet prairie, sit at its feet
that it might set me on fire. Then I'll go back,
ignite one mind, one heart with one spark.

*Job 12:7-8
**Li Po

IN THE COMPANY OF ALLIGATORS

They were the last thing
I went to see—could not imagine
what the attraction could be.
I went for birds: anhingas,
spoonbills, egrets, herons.
And swamp lilies.

Manatees and dark, steamy
mangroves. Maritime fauna.
Palmetto palms and pig frogs.
Whispering of wind across
sawgrass prairies. But then
I spotted that first one dozing

along Anhinga Trail, and
I was hooked. Hearing
the bellowing of two echoing
across the slough—a sutra—
I knew they were saints
if not prophets, beyond good

and evil, soul-readers seeing by
God's light, wildly created,
audacious, hypnotic, driven
forward by practicalities—not
hostilities, in control—rulers but
not dictators of the slough, kings

of the vast river of grass, a dark
tense presence, unadulterated motion
among soft-shelled turtles, garfish

and fallen ripened pond apples.
Sinking deep into my awareness,
triumphantly fulfilling my need

for distinct, unabashed wildness.
Back now in my desert, the Everglades
flows through my days,
bellows of alligators like plain chants
echo in my ears—rhapsody, love song
so endearing, drowning out the groaners

of this sad world. Hosanna
to the alligators in the highest:
Glory be to their Maker.

BEGGAR IN THE EVERGLADES

It pierces my heart till I rejoice when the mosquito pricks my finger for blood to nurture her eggs, initiating me into the life cycle of this place to which I've come like meeting someone for the first time and feeling I've known her my whole life. They tell me their life story, and I'm converted—born again— their waters, slow-moving shallow river rising with summer rain, baptize me. And I'm forgiven—sins of omission (failing to do the little I could do to protect and restore them)— draining, bull-dozing of their saw grass prairies. Washed in the blood of a million plume birds, I offer my body to be bitten, slashed, burned, but they neither punish nor scold; they are gentle, delicate even in their pain, in their sentient struggle to regain their rightful place. Sovereign in tenacity, endurance of extremes: drought, deluge, plenty, starvation, disaster. They are the sisters I never had—graceful, brave, beautiful. Symbol of fortitude, rainbow after the storm. Stasis in the mangroves, pivot of manatee and speedboat. I walk softly, silently—afraid of killing, injuring, disturbing anything in this fragile place. Red-winged blackbird taking over my favorite post and alligator dozing on my path remind me I'm the intruder—here today, gone tomorrow; they have been, will be, here forever. I lift up my cup and bowl for them to fill, walk humbly through sword-sharp sawgrass by the slough, admiring the slender visions heaven-made: egret, heron, anhinga, ibis, wood stork, bittern, limpkin. Bowing before them, I pray for their flame that I might burn through the dark night and give light. Their flight and calls like elaborate alternations of Quranic recitations and mystical music. Let a green bird—heron preferred—descend on my head if indeed I am the elect. Let me make collyrium for my eyes from the dust kicked up by the alligator, that I might see more clearly and die pure. Let the master mixer of the red sulphur elixir, the roseate spoonbill, transform my soul into pure gold. Then, great egret white and delicate as falling snow, send me forth as arrow to pierce hearts set on destruction.

EXISTENCE IS LIGHT

What will the world be once bereft
of wet and wildness? Let them be left.
—Gerard Manley Hopkins

Nowhere have I heard it more clearly,
Beginning's Word, past still being spoken
by alligator and whippoorwill. Nowhere

have I seen as radiant a light as that
reflecting off tawny sawgrass where
that master of illumination, great white heron,
stands in the niche for lights.

I've traveled to Aleppo and studied
theosophical Sufism, but only in the Everglades
did it finally make sense: existence is light—

light equally illuminating green and brown.
Slogging in my Wellingtons across prairie
through moat onto hardwood hammock where
the strangler fig launched a shimmering seed at me,

the five-lined skink shined metallic blue
as light called it forth out of its slumber,
I vowed to remain silent and celibate

if I could end my days among Sufi master
snowy egret, angel roseate spoonbill,
the hunched Han poet green heron. I'd
stay awake, I'd meditate—let the light

illuminate life moving above and through
the river of grass. I would not ask
for rain in dry season—only for light,

and to enter into the wildness and wet—
to do nothing more or less than reflect
it as perfectly as the snowy egret's three-
egged nest braced on a cardinal airplant

proliferating on a dwarf cypress.

ELEGY FOR GUY BRADLEY, 1870-1905*

Braving hoards of mosquitoes along the trail named for him—
neglected since Katrina wreaked havoc here—I walk solemnly
beside a mangrove-lined shore bordering a former fishing
village named for birds driven away by plume hunters. One
Snowy egret just off-shore reminding me not to forget what he
died for. Protected from mid-day sun by a green safari hat—far
cry from the fancy bonnets those women of the Gilded Age
craved, I pay homage on the Everglades' southeastern fringe to
the victims of the Plume Wars—one Audubon game warden,
the egrets and herons—five million a year by 1886, thanks to
the hottest hats adorned with aigrettes—nuptial plumes of
the Snowy egret. Was my great-grandmother a culprit? Trail
of bloody slaughter, human greed—how could women lower
themselves to need such frills? Plume hunters with Winchester
.22 rifles and silent Floberts, moonshine and chewing tobacco
shooting out whole rookeries in a day. Crime after crime,
leaving behind dying fledgling birds. I could almost forgive
them—men putting food on family tables. But those fashion-
conscious women? Never. That was the Age, the craze, of
Extermination: doomed Carolina parakeet, Passenger pigeon,
buffalo shot from moving trains—left to rot on the plains.
Alligators and birds on the banks of Florida's rivers shot from
steamboats. The one I could have loved stood guarding the
rookery deep in a mangrove swamp. I am the sentry standing
now on the verge of Florida Bay, Flamingo Village, daring any
modern-day man to pillage this sacred place where baby egrets
and herons watched mothers being murdered, then slowly
starved. I am here now, I whisper to his spirit lingering on this
shore, ready to fight though I admit my fear and bafflement as
I walk in this most sacred, profane place of bitter battles over
game bird hunting, wondering about the nature of women

and men—crusader knights to Yankee Doodle adorning their heads with feathers and plumes. Curse prosperous times and advertising ploys, plume hunters and buyers, traders and salesmen, millinery workers, fashion designers. Bless Frank Chapman for counting Manhattan's winter birds perched atop Macy's fashion plates, 1886. Bless George Bird Grinnell for creating the first Audubon Society. Bless Guy Bradley for defending to the death America's most precious endangered rookery. Looking across Florida Bay to a small island surrounded by mangroves, I envision droves of plume birds—egrets, herons—and Guy waving to me.

*Audubon game warden killed in line of duty protecting egret rookeries from plume poachers turn of 19th-century; 1st martyr to America's environmental movement.

GRASSY RIVER

We need the tonic of wildness . . . to witness . . .
some life pasturing freely where we never wander.
—Henry David Thoreau

Needy, I came to the wet prairies
where at dawn I listened to bird songs
in pineland, sawgrass, hammocks,
cypress swamps. At dusk to cacophonous

Cricket, Green, Little Grass and Pig frogs
in Taylor Slough. Watched alligators,
gar, Soft-shelled turtles do
what their ancestors did. Stood

apart at the edge of the grassy river,
watching with my whole heart, the air
quivering with a wildness I didn't dare
touch. Rejoiced in the mystery. So much

we can't know. Clearly
herons, ibis, egrets were fishing;
could they be guarding as well
their watery domain from invaders

who envisioned it drained
for farmland and suburban sprawl?
Learned all about its changing
landscape and peoples—

Paleo, Archaic Indian, Calusa,
the Spaniards—how the derelict land
was made (contours of its bedrock,
thickness of its soils), how restoration began.

Needy, I witnessed mangroves shielding

the shoreline the day I walked there
alone with one Red-shouldered hawk
keeping watch from its Royal palm throne,

and that Swallow-tailed kite soaring
above a cypress dome. And the silence,
the timelessness in which herons,
ibis and egrets graze their grassy river.

OFF-SEASON IN PARADISE

Soft-shelled turtles
seeming imperturbable
in Taylor Slough.
Lubber grasshoppers
making their way by day
to the String lilies.

Solitary Rockland morning glory
telling its ancient story
of endangerment.
The orb weaver spinning
its golden silk between two
Sabal palm fronds.

Zebras fluttering as if floating
on the margins of hardwood hammocks.
After dark, moonflowers scenting
mangroves, attracting Hawk moths
in droves.

And Ghost orchids drawing deep
into their cypress swamps
the Giant Sphinx.
Dragonflies—pennants,
green darners, pondhawks,
blue dashers—and Common

nighthawks feeding
on a million mosquitoes.
Around shallow pond edges

and flooded depressions,
Little Grass, Green and Pig frogs—

someone's playing marbles:
hear the click-clicking of
Cricket frogs. A lamb bleating
on a rainy night: Eastern Narrow-
mouthed frog.

How utterly odd, how sublime
hordes of tourists are gone
at this most magical time.

ENVIOUS

Perhaps we should hire the poets instead of the biologists to write our science textbooks!
—Steve van Matre

On this third planet from the sun,
in the western hemisphere,
on the Florida Platform,
at the edge of an interior
freshwater marsh . . .
                                   No, let me start over:
In this month of June,
at the beginning of rainy season,
in the year of the Lord 2007 . . .
                                   Still not right. One more time:
These June mornings I walk out
to watch the sun rise over a sawgrass marsh.
I criss-cross Taylor Slough full of alligators,
soft-shelled turtles, gar fish and such—
everything so exotic I want to hold on
but don't dare touch. I've come,
drawn to edges: a continent,
North America, peninsular Florida,
sawgrass prairie, mangroves. I've come
to learn from the endangered ones:
West Indian manatee, Florida panther,
Wood stork, American crocodile—to
sit a long while at the edge of their coastal
mangrove swamps, shallow estuaries,
hardwood hammocks.

These June dusks I walk out
to watch the sun sink into a grassy river.
I criss-cross Taylor Slough with my entourage
of dragonflies clearing the path of mosquitoes.
I watch how they all live side by side—

alligator, turtle, fish—taking only enough
to survive, how they harmonize together
each in his or her own dialect: the frogs—
Cricket, Little Grass, Green and Pig;
the waders—heron, egret, limpkin, ibis.

Watching, listening, oblivious
to self till I realize I'm envious.

CELESTIAL CATHEDRAL

Heaven is under our feet as well as over our heads.
—Henry David Thoreau

Every configuration
of cloud and mangrove,
each endangered Cape Sable
Seaside sparrow, Florida

panther, manatee,
crocodile, hardwood
hammock, slough.
Disguised angels:

ibis, heron, egret shining
light on sawgrass prairies,
lending hallelujahs and
mandolas at dusk to frogs.

No barren soil—epiphytes
feeding on nothing but air and
sunlight, growing on mahogany
and Pond apple trees.

Alligators and Roseate spoonbills
revealing a place wounded by man,
forgiving as rain falls
from the upper chamber.

RETURNING

We are nature, long have we been absent,
but now we return.
—Walt Whitman

Never to be quite the same, I came
to the Everglades. Once one has
walked alone at dusk among alligators,
how to ever again content oneself
among one's own species? Once
Meister Eckhart's words sink in,

as they will when you linger with one
Roseate spoonbill, *Nothing in all*
creation is so like God as stillness,
how to resume a safe speed?
Hushed by harmonies of Little Grass,
Green and Cricket frogs, stopped

in one's tracks by Soft-shelled turtles
nibbling on Spatterdock leaves and
Pond apples, consoled along footpaths
and boardwalks through mangroves and those
hardwood hammocks harboring the last
of the great mahoganies, one senses

an eternal recompense, a peace
both cause and goal of creation—
Everglades made of primordial love.
But then the ships came in—
hauled away egrets' and spoonbills'
plumes. Fledglings left to starve,

whole rookeries decimated.
As pilgrim kneeling where a game
warden was murdered protecting them,

Indians enslaved and slaughtered,
Jesuit priests martyred, I return,
am nature now, and I grieve.

AMERICAN ALLIGATOR

Who could be so hard-
hearted, so blind not to see
this is their world,

not ours? Look how they
float together now, May,
summer rains beginning,

diving with flexible air tanks,
touching noses from time
to time as sun and showers

move across their slough.
Ripe Pond apples plopping
into it just for them—

most advanced of all reptiles.
Bellows of eligible ones
echoing edge to edge,

deep and rumbling, announcing
this is their turf—you nothing
more than an afterthought

on this earth. World lighter
because of their stalwart energy
outshining Gen-X brainiacs.

EVERGLADES' KEYSTONE SPECIES

If you understand nature, you will never be afraid or alone.
—Rachel Carson

Because I trusted she was right,
I walked alone along Anhinga Trail
over Taylor Slough every dusk for one
month among alligators, fearing one thing
only: the lone man, cigarette dangling
from lips, disregarding the *No Smoking* sign
posted at the entrance, who didn't fit
the profile—tourist/nature lover.

How liberating to discover
alligators can be quite companionable,
though a bit shy and elusive at times.
What I wish for you is this:
that you might inhabit this poem—
feel the thrill, slight chill of fear
creeping up the spine as you (go on,
take my place) walk alone past the lounging
alligator that has sidled up the bank
of the slough to stretch out on the cool
summer grass beside the walking path,
and now is casually watching you pass by.

That you might politely give him space,
resist the urge to thrust a camera in his face—
that together you two might watch the sun sink
into *his* sawgrass prairie beyond *his* slough. That you
might linger, listening as he tells how his living
flowing realm is all there is—how it sings
through him, how he lives in it without greed,
eating on average once a week what he needs
to subsist—how even if he were hungry now

you're really not his cup of tea—
much too large and meaty.

That you might stay there as the hesitant moon
rises over the slough to reflect in the eyes of all
the drowsy alligators, that you'll notice a lack
of fierceness in them—see only curiosity,
contentment, not a hint of animosity. That you,
with your two feet, might walk gently on their
holy ground, thanking them for gracious
hospitality, thanking their creator for such
an exemplary keystone species.

IF YOU DOUBT

If you doubt,
go out to where
Snowy egret stands
among Swamp lilies.
Wait silent and still

like it, and listen
as each frog
takes up its chant.
Watch how sun sinks
into sawgrass marsh,

and the afterglow
smoothes out the slough's
rough edges.
Watch Mother Alligator
guarding her young

though they have flung
themselves far and wide
just now. Listen:
Green heron scolding them;
watch how he leans

toward the dark waters,
spits out a Pond apple bit—
luring a Killifish.
Notice when Snowy egret
spears a Grass frog,

silence reigns as Creation,
in unison, awaits the light
of a new day when nothing
will kill in Her holy slough
and sawgrass marsh.

MERCURY

A quiet peaceful day.
A lone alligator yawns,
passing under the boardwalk.
Cuban Knight anole, pale pink
throat fan ballooning out, lays

in wait for a fly to light nearby.
Little Green heron perched just
above the slough keeps watch
for a Sailfin molly. A 'gator
hole within a cypress head

entices deer to come browse
Pickerelweed whose lavender
blue flowers, just at their peak,
captivate Peacock butterflies.
Five-lined skink, metallic-blue,

pauses to drink from a wild pine's
cup-like leaf. Two mating alligators
toss and turn on the grassy bank—
each time I circle around, they're found
in a new coupling position.

Pig frogs camouflaged
among floating lilies. Peaceful,
quiet day gives way to night
that mirrors it, mercury creeping
menacingly up the food chain.

EDGE OF A SAWGRASS PRAIRIE

Golden green in setting sunlight, sedges
shimmer as soft rain falls. Black bird
once dull now glows iridescently purple.
A Tri-colored heron stands in dark blue-grey
contrast beside an all-white morph.
The symphony begins—stereo sound,
cinematography in the round: bleating
Narrowmouthed frogs on the left; marble-

clicking Cricket frogs on the right;
grunting Pig frogs hunting crayfish;
rumble of two alligators vying for their
favorite resting place. Binoculars and
umbrella forgotten, I walk awestruck,
grateful for my stroke of good luck—
not another human around. One skulking Green-
backed heron swoops down to check me out—

so close I hear its wings flapping.
Baby alligators surface and stare, curious
as to why I'm way up there. At peace
in the midst of all this wildness, I ponder
prisoners plotting escapes, aging parents
housebound, myself pacing a classroom nine
months a year. Caged in—all of our wings
clipped by society, tradition, religion. Free now,

I bask in just enough remaining light to ignite
the Lubber grasshopper making its way from
Swamp lily leaves to its bed. Enough light
to detect the cardinal at the tree island's edge,

two green Pond apples ready to fall, Soft-
shelled turtle just below the surface, ready to feast.
One must stay alert—attentive to margins,
shallows, uppermost branches. Take chances,

forsake everything familiar, and though partial
to ocean, explore where one's never gone before:
sawgrass marsh, wet prairie, slough.
Too soon one's time on Earth is through.
Leave now, you can make it for tomorrow's
performance—same time, same venue.
As for me, I'm flying off to Cape Sable if
weather permits and I'm physically able.

EVERGLADES HISTORY LESSON ONE

First the Calusas, Mayaimis,
Tekestas came—living on fish and game,
fashioning tools out of seashells.

Then Spanish Conquistadors—
and Tekestas, Mayaimis were no more.
Only Calusas, scattered, remained.
But the Spaniards didn't stay—
frightened away by razor-sharp ridged
sedge and squalling alligators.

Next, the Creeks—Muskogee-
speaking people from the west—
and Seminoles, kicked out of
the Carolinas by European invaders.

Then white hunters massacring two million
egrets and Roseate spoonbills for breeding
feathers to adorn women's hats, killing
alligators for hides to craft shoes and wallets.

Then engineers digging canals, draining
fresh water to make farmland and towns.

Finally pesticides, fertilizers flowing
into the waters, poisoning one-celled
animals, snails, mammals, fish,
birds and plants. Doesn't everyone wish

for a happy ending? Endangered ecosystem
restored to its splendor? Swamp lily,

Calopogon orchid thriving? Crocodile,
Liguus tree snail, Green anole surviving
to extol the Everglades' glory—its central
solitudes holding fast time's secrets?

Doesn't everyone hope beyond all
hope Jeremiah heard wrong?*

*Jeremiah 4:23-28

KIN TO ALL OF NATURE

Surrounded by the grassy river, finally
becoming *plants, trunks, foliage, roots, bark,*
I caught Walt Whitman's meaning.

Became a coral, a sponge at home
on the hard marine bottom, a succulent
on a coastal prairie beyond the mudflats.

Became the tallest conifer of a cypress dome,
quite at home in standing water.

Became the twirled strangler fig on a gumbo limbo,
peeling bark the trunk curled back in protest,
acid from a decaying plant dissolving limestone
around a hardwood hammock, helping make the moat.

Became soil collecting in the jagged bedrock,
root of a slash pine taking its time breaking through
the crack, the outer bark of the pine scorched by fire
sweeping across a limestone ridge.

Became one blade of golden green sawgrass
swaying as if praying for one songbird
to perch and sing its praises to sky and prairie.

Became the haven of shade in the hum
of the hammock, the five-lined teal-tailed skink
poised on the rail, listening and waiting.

Became the wide grassy river, wetness
of summer, seagrass sheltering shellfish.

Became a coastal channel, mangrove forest,
stilt-like roots of one red mangrove.

Became marl sediment settled
on the limestone of a freshwater prairie,
allowing slow seepage of water.

Became the deeper faster-flowing center
of that broad marshy river, panther
prowling on hidden hammocks through
the night, thunder cloud spilling out
its blessing summer afternoons.

Became alligator sunning on Taylor Slough's bank,
pond apple plopping into the silently flowing,
rising river, zebra swallowtail dreaming
on the string lily, fanning my wings.

Became water defying human borders—
vapor moving invisibly,
liquid percolating through peaty soil and marl.

Became myself again as I once was
in the beginning—present to and kin to
all of nature.

PA-HAY-OKEE*

Grassy waters beguiled me
(too long caught up in black holes,
exploding stars, the mystical sphere)
back down to Earth: sawgrasses;
and between blades, an ever so
slowly rising, flowing river—

Earth's circulatory system draining
into the Gulf of Mexico, Atlantic
Ocean, evaporating back into
the atmosphere, water composed
of alligators' tears. Cladium jamaicense
swaying and setting tiny sharp teeth

against the rainy season's wind.
Courageous egrets tip-toeing
through shiny saw-toothed edges
of golden-green sedges.
Swamp lilies trembling among
gar and anhingas. Lingered

among them, endangered
if need be as the ones struggling
to survive: Cape Sable
Seaside sparrow, West Indian
manatee, Wood stork,
Florida panther,

Indigo snake, American
crocodile, Apple snail

in this massive watershed—
America's largest sawgrass
prairie—where I came
back down to Earth.

*The Seminole Indians called the Everglades Pa-hay-
okee, meaning grassy waters.

TATTERED BATTLEFIELD, NATIONAL TREASURE

Hell's roof,
heaven's floor,
the last depository before

emptying into the ocean.
Wetlands once labeled
wastelands—unfarmable,

unsailable—worthless morass,
useless bog, haunt of noxious
vermin: mosquitoes,

rattlesnakes, alligators.
Still the dreamers and schemers
came with their cacophonous

fracases—attempted to drain
and tame it. But it fought back.
Took revenge: devastating droughts,

ferocious floods and winds,
horrendous hurricanes warning
Mother Nature wasn't happy.

Wasteland to fantasyland,
half of it gone, why can't man
understand this is no way to live—

taming rivers, draining swamps.
All Mother Nature really wants
is a redress of harmony—restoration

of clean water: trinity of timing,
delivery, quantity—put everything
back in order as we found it

in the beginning.

TOGETHER WE WATCH

Every dusk I stay with her
awhile, offer some semblance
of camaraderie. How feeble
I must seem, unable to dive

deep and impale a bream—
no stiletto beak, no poking beneath
spatterdock leaves for sunfish and bass,
no wings to fly up to the tip

of a willow thicket and keep watch
over Taylor Slough. If only I knew
why she stayed behind.
Together we watch two alligators

roll and rumble, listen
to their mating bellows, then
watch one float away log-like
to the Pond apples. Together—

anhinga clinging with stubby webbed
feet to willow branch, one human leaning
on boardwalk railing—we watch
Great egrets fly over, thunder

clouds gather. When I whisper,
I'm poised to fly, if I just had wings . . .
she doesn't stir. But I sense her
sigh of comprehension.

MURDER IN THE EVERGLADES
(or THE EVERGLADES STRANGLER)

Ficus aurea, of West Indies origin,
wetland resident of tree islands,

common hammock tree, can you see
me admiring you even as you choke

to death this gumbo limbo,
your roots proliferating downward

toward forest floor? And what's more,
there—in the head of that cabbage

palm—one seed just beginning its life
as an epiphyte.

You, dear strangler fig, kill ever
so softly by dense shade—

not like man, with his pesticide
and blade.

SHARK VALLEY

Like a protective mother,
I stand on the canal bank—
daring any predator to touch it
as it sleeps on drifting dried debris
of reeds and willow tree. Oh
I well know its real mother,

hidden, is watching it and me
closely. All around, sound of
garfish flipping and splashing
pellucid waters for oxygen.
Baby doesn't flinch or open its
eyes, mesmerized by the rocking

of its reedy raft, warm midday sun,
steady insect hum. Modest
hairstreaks drink from purple phlox
while I roast and sweat. But I remain
because I know the odds: never again
to find myself alone on a canal bank

watching over a one-foot-long baby
alligator, never to feel as much motherly
instinct as if I'd birthed it. So I stay,
unwilling to walk away from the most
placid, endearing sight I'll see all day,
unwilling to share it with bypassing

tourists so busy talking they don't even
notice, wondering if it's right to turn

eventually to inkpots and canvases—even
with childlike abandon, even if I daub in
just enough color and shape to suggest
Elysium.

SHARK VALLEY, NEAR NOON

Of what avail is an open eye if the heart is blind?
—Solomon Ibn Gabirol

Headwaters, western edge of Shark
River Slough. From lavender blue
spikes of pickerelweed, Silver-spotted
skippers seek nectar.

One female anhinga, having speared
a bream with its stiletto beak, now beats
it against a willow branch, flips it once,
twice; now swallows it whole;
goes back down for another.

The other species seem less energetic—
Mud turtle, Killifish, Spotted bass
and gars, tilapia, Blue gills.

Voracious full-grown alligators
lethargic in mid-day sun: one's
horny plates glistening; the other's
dried out. Near noon, no bellow.
all is mesmerizingly mellow.

A bayhead called Bobcat, fragrant
with floriferous trees: Magnolia
Virginiana, Red bay.

Across the sawgrass and marl prairie,
no sign of Wood stork nor Snail kite.
Only Little Blue and Tri-colored herons,
one young ibis, Red-winged blackbirds,
one killdeer, one Red-shouldered hawk.

In a borrow pit, an apple snail.
Along Otter Cave Trail, exposed
limestone substrate in the hardwood
hammock. Was that a White Peacock?

Keep looking. Harder.
Longer. Below surfaces.
Rainy season—even near noon,
no end to the vibrancy.

FIRST SUNSET, ANHINGA TRAIL

Dragonflies—Four-spotted and Halloween Pennants, Eastern Pondhawks and Blue Dashers—were my escorts, feasting on the mosquitoes that would have feasted on me. Alligators lay quietly dozing, all but two who were swimming from pond apples to willow thicket. One Red-winged blackbird landed right on the railing to which I was heading, one foot away, as if to say, *This is my spot for sunset*, and I couldn't blame him—it was the best seat in the house as the sun lowered itself behind sawgrass. The trail criss-crosses Taylor Slough, and if you go at dusk you may luck out and be the only human there. But you won't be alone or lonely. If you wait patiently, a pond apple will fall and make a splash that attracts the Red-bellied turtle whose crunching attracts the alligator if he hasn't had his weekly fill of Florida gar. If you walk slowly, softly, Limpkin won't flee when you approach. She'll study you as intently as you study her in the gloam while the choruses of Little Grass, Cricket, Green Tree and Pig frogs erupt from all sides. And Eastern Narrow-mouthed frogs repeat their sheeplike bleats. Limpkin will stay near you till she's distracted by the plaintive childlike wailing of one of her own kind. Then she'll fly off into the sawgrass, and for a moment you'll feel a stab of loneliness, but it won't last long—not if you allow yourself to get caught up in the frogs' songs, and you notice the dozing alligators all around you, and of course the dragonflies, which as I said before have cleared the way so you are walking as if in paradise, nothing harming you. And, becoming overwhelmed by a sense of your own insignificance, you find it liberating, intoxicating; you feel, for the first time in the longest time, utterly at peace here in the midst of wild things. Surely this slough, this willow thicket, this sawgrass marsh resembles—if it is not in fact—paradise, while just beside it, the Gumbo Limbo Trail, though lush and exotic, looms like a corner of hell, with its insatiable, inescapable mosquitoes—not a dragonfly around.

FACING ARIDITY

Do not divert your love from visible things. But go on loving what is good, simple and ordinary—animals and flowers, and keep the balance true.
—Rainer Maria Rilke

Home again, I unpack the sounds,
close my eyes and listen till I'm back
among anhingas, little green and cricket
frogs, bellowing alligators, a thunderstorm.

First one set aside to preserve biological
(not geological) resources, it'll flow now
through my veins like honey, like
streams in a desert—in this dot of a desert,

finger pointing into the Arabian Sea.
Everglades nourishing me as it does
wading birds in the sawgrass sea,
fresh water meandering southward

toward Florida Bay.
Back among Islamic mosaics,
I now treasure another kind: of
ponds and sloughs, hardwood

hammocks, sawgrass marshes—
fragile wetlands for endangered
manatee, Wood stork, Florida panther,
Cape Sable seaside sparrow.

Thunder peals as ibis, herons,
spoonbills spill over Eco Pond.
Subtropical wonderland sounds
to refresh my withering soul.

National treasure, delicate
ecosystem of unsurpassable
diversity, help me face aridity
and keep the balance true.

Diana Woodcock's Everglades-inspired poetry was chosen in 2013 to be part of Fresh AIRE: Artists' Experiences in a World Heritage Site: a traveling exhibition (Artists-in-Residence in the Everglades), as well as to be featured in the Through Your Eyes Web Multimedia Exhibitions of the National Parks Service. Several poems were selected for the O, Miami Poetry Festival (April 2011) and for the Everglades National Park's special AIRIE (Artists in Residence in Everglades) exhibit at the Ernest F. Coe Visitor Center (December 2011). She is the author of *Under the Spell of a Persian Nightingale* and *Swaying on the Elephant's Shoulders,* which won the 2010 Vernice Quebodeaux International Poetry Prize for Women. Her chapbooks include *Desert Ecology: Lessons and Visions, Tamed by the Desert, In the Shade of the Sidra Tree, Mandala,* and *Travels of a Gwai Lo.* Widely published in literary journals, her poems have been nominated for the Pushcart Prize and Best of the Net Award. Her award-winning poem, "Music as Scripture," was performed onstage in Lincoln Park, San Francisco in 2014 by Natica Angilly's Poetic Dance Theater Company at Artists Embassy International's 21st Dancing Poetry Festival. A PhD candidate at Lancaster University, she currently teaches at Virginia Commonwealth University in Qatar. Previously, she lived and worked in Tibet, Macau and Thailand.